MOZART

CONCERTO No. 5
"TURKISH"
in A major, K. 219

FOR VIOLIN AND PIANO

Edited and provided with Cadenzas
by JOSEPH JOACHIM

Published in 2019 by Allegro Editions

Concerto No. 5 "Turkish" for Violin and Piano
ISBN: 978-1-9748-9967-8 (paperback)

Cover design by Kaitlyn Whitaker

Cover image: "Violin Front View Isolated on White" by AGCuesta, courtesy of Shutterstock;
"Black and White Piano Keys" by Nerthuz, courtesy of iStock;
"Music Sheet" by danielo, courtesy of Shutterstock

ALLEGRO EDITIONS

CONCERTO No. 5
in A major, K. 219, "Turkish"
for Violin and Piano

Edited by JOSEPH JOACHIM

WOLFGANG AMADEUS MOZART
(1756-1791)

RONDO
Tempo di Minuetto (♩ circa 126)

CADENZA by JOACHIM

CONCERTO No. 5
"TURKISH"
in A major, for Violin and Piano

PART FOR VIOLIN

CONCERTO No. 5
in A major, K. 219, "Turkish"
for Violin and Piano

VIOLIN

Edited and with Cadenzas by
JOSEPH JOACHIM

WOLFGANG AMADEUS MOZART
(1756-1791)

attacca

40

www.ingramcontent.com/pod-product-compliance
Lightning Source LLC
LaVergne TN
LVHW061344060426
835512LV00016B/2658